Rooks at the I

- the Rooks of Stonehenge

By

Carol Druce

ANCES-CAWS

The featherless ones, Joe thought to himself, had no proper sense of migration. Not like the swallows who, after an initial herald or two, arrived all together and left together. The featherless had the instinct to travel, he acknowledged. They seemed to be drawn to Stonehenge. That he could understand. That he felt himself. Some arrived in small flocks, on things they called coaches. Others came in cars, in dribs and drabs. But they arrived at Stonehenge whatever the time of year, whatever the weather. He wondered whether they learnt from their ancestors where the safe places were, the places with water, food and shelter, the way he had learnt from his. He wondered where they roosted at night.

They provided easy food. Rooks had always followed people for easy food, Joe mused. His distant ancestors had followed the first stone age hunters, picking clean the discarded carcasses of their spoils. The featherless ones rarely noticed them. Their caws were part of the soundscape - but camouflaged within their caws to this day, was the faintest echo of a Palaeolithic axe, from the time when the featherless first used stone tools.

Now it was from the café that Joe found pickings. He sat on the fence post, watching, waiting for it to open. Cars were bringing the first of the featherless ones. They called themselves custodians of the great stone circle of Stonehenge but Joe knew it was really the jackdaws, his smaller cousins, who were the guardians. They nested under the horizontal stones held high on the uprights and taught their young the secrets of the stones, handed down from their ancestors.

Arrival of the featherless ones meant there would soon be biscuits for breakfast. He waited until he saw them go through the shop door and then he flew onto the metal perching post, conveniently located between the shop and the entrance. From this vantage point, he would be able to personally greet all the visitors - and hopefully get snacks.

"Caw!" he said and one of the featherless brought him a piece of biscuit. Apparently they were for visitors, who spread them with jam sold in the shop to see if they liked it. Joe preferred his biscuit without jam.

ALL CHANGE

Something had been going on for months. First, cars stopped travelling passed Stonehenge to park in its car park. They came and left the same way. The road was filled in and grassed over. This did not affect Joe and delivery of his snacks but it was unsettling. But one morning there were no cars, no featherless ones. Eventually they arrived by bus. Then the visitors started to come on the same buses. Lots of people were walking along the road and through the fields. Strangest of all, the café remained shut and shuttered. Something peculiar had clearly happened. Joe flew to the trees where he could see where the buses came from and went to - the new Stonehenge Visitors' Centre. From his vantage point, Joe sidled to the end of the branch and snapped off a fat twig. He flew with it round the field - rounding up a few of his peers. He led them to a tree and they settled in its branches. Joe carefully put his stick down.

"Caw!" Joe spoke first. "We have a crisis."

"Should we relocate to this new structure?"

"And leave our stones!"

"Caw - no! Caw - no! Caw - no!"

Joe picked up his stick and they all flew away.

By the next day, Joe found to his joy that one of the featherless ones was at the stones, feeding the jackdaws who lived amongst stones. It was not the same though. The jackdaws were on a healthy eating plan and were fed bird food. He preferred junk food.

Soon the bus drivers started to feed him too. He liked sitting on the wing mirrors for snacks. It was not the same as the food he had from the café. He thought fondly of the time when a flock of schoolchildren had arrived with fish and chips and there had been leftovers for rooks. The fish had been exceedingly tasty.

Joe went to the stones less and less.

BO

Bo was the most beautiful of rooks. Son of Joe, real rook royalty, so the other rooks deferred to him. He was kind and wise and never bullied the younger rooks. He would show them who was boss by ruffling his head feathers, bending his neck and spreading his tail feathers like a peacock.

He knew he was safe with the featherless one who fed the jackdaws and would follow her whenever he felt like a snack, bouncing along beside her as she walked round the stones. He was happy to catch food too but it felt a bit undignified, jumping into the air to catch and so he preferred to take the food from her hand, he knew it was just for him.

BELLE AND HER CHICKS

Belle was worn out trying to feed her two growing chicks. She knew there was easy food to be got from the featherless one, so as soon as they could fly away from their twig cradles high in the tree tops, she took them to the stones. She landed on the patch of grass behind the featherless one. The two chicks, Albie and Alfie, followed her all day long but at least she did not have to keep flying back and forth with food for them.

She was not the only mum who had the same idea. Soon another mum started bringing her chick - the noisiest youngster, who screeched all day at her mum for food. The predominant sound around the monument all that summer was her screeching. On account of her moaning, she was named Mona.

PARLIAMENT

A flock of rooks from the field beyond the fence flew over the stones. The rooks and jackdaws immediately took wing to see them out of their territory. They set up a loud cawing and clamouring. Albie flew up with his mum and brother. When all settled down, he returned in time to overhear one of the visitors asking a featherless one what a group of rooks was called.

"There are lots of different names. Clamour's one - like you've just heard! A storytelling too - because when they're roosting or nesting they sound like they're telling one another stories. I guess the best known one is a parliament."

Albie shuddered. He had heard that word before. He had once overheard his mum and dad talking about a parliament. Belle had sounded a bit scared. He had asked her what it was.

"Nothing you need to know about yet. It's something that happens to very bad rooks. You're a good little rook. When you grow up you'll learn the code of laws in our rookery." He didn't ask again but listened to the adults talking. He understood that a parliament was taking place between the rooks and that grandfather Joe was there. Like all curious teenagers, he had flown to the very top of the trees with other juvenile rooks to try and see what was going on. In a distant field, they could see a circle of rooks with one sitting quietly in the centre, head down. Albie could not see what was happening and got bored after a while. Some while later he flew up again and it didn't look as though any of the rooks had moved. He watched briefly, puzzled. Shortly after, grandfather Joe flew back. His beak was bloodied and he looked sad.

"Had to be done," he muttered. Albie flew up to the top of the tree again. In the distance the only thing showing any sign of life were a few feathers lifting in the breeze. He never discovered what crime had been committed but justice had been dispensed, rook fashion.

A ROOK ROMANCE

By the following spring, Mona had discovered she was expected to feed herself and that her mum was too busy canoodling with her dad to feed her. She was not happy with this, so she looked around for someone who might be coerced into providing her with snacks. Albie had always been a bit of a softie - and he was rook royalty. His grandfather was the legendary Joe, top of the roosting perch, top in the pecking order. She turned her full attention to him. He was a very handsome young rook, she thought. They both still had tufts of black feathers round their beaks. She thought his were very cute. They would not loose them until the following autumn. Now they were teenage rooks, they had grown flying feathers that were blues and browns as well as black.

Albie liked the attention he got from Mona. He liked the way she glanced at him when she thought he was not looking. He knew how much she liked her food so he decided to make her a present of the next tasty morsel he found.

Albie soon grew to love Mona dearly but she needed a lot of looking after. Spoilt by her mum, who had indulged her every whim, she demanded the same attention from Albie. So she squawked at him from sunrise till sunset. Albie quickly learnt that the closer he got to the featherless one, the more food he got. He even took it from her hand, like he had seen grandfather Joe doing.

One day he was feeling very impatient. He sat on the rope fence behind Featherless looking to see what she had in her hand. It was full of tasty suet. That should keep Mona quiet. Albie didn't wait. He flew onto her hand and helped himself. She was so enchanted that she kept getting more food out for him.

At last his crop was full and flew on to the grass to feed Mona, filling her beak with suet from his pouch. A romantic meal, rook style.

"I think you're cl-awesome," he whispered.

"You're very win-g-some," she whispered back.

CATCHING AND CACHING

Sometimes the rooks sat on the grass behind the featherless one. They knew she would always throw food to the jackdaws, so they made sure they stayed close to them. Sometimes she threw food for them to catch. They were all very good at catching - they had had a lot of practice. Albie did not like sharing and it was never very long before he flew onto her hand.

"Aw! Aw! Aw!" he called as he arrived.

Albie liked the attention he got when he flew onto the featherless one's hand. He liked that people crowded round him, taking his photo. Sometimes he gathered quite a crowd. He always got extra food when he modelled. Occasionally he took food from the visitors if they had something tasty for him.

Of-course, he could not eat all the food he was given so then he took it into the field, dug a hole with his beak and hid the contents of his pouch in it, to return to on the days the featherless one was not there to feed him. If he thought another rook was watching, he pretended to hide it but then flew off and dug a different hole. He did it with his beak open, like a compass set. He knew there was a special word for his digging. It was called zirkelning, from the German word for compass. He did it when he was digging for grubs, too.

Sometimes when he had eaten his fill, Albie was content to sit on the featherless one's hand. He made a soft noise, which was something between a purr and a song. It was a very contented sound.

There were times he could not fit all the food into his pouch. Then he would regurgitate it into the hand of the featherless one before rearranging it. She did get a bit of a surprise on the day when he dropped a worm into her hand, which had been neatly coiled in his beak.

THE PIED ONE

As the days cooled and daylight shortened, the time when the veils between the worlds thinned, the rooks moved from their twig homes in the rookery to their winter roost in amongst pine trees. There was more shelter there during the cold winter months. Through the long evenings there was storytelling, stories of long ago, of their ancestors who watched the stones of Stonehenge being raised. During the day they flew to their usual feeding areas. Most of the rooks were part of a small group, each of whom had their own territory.

Several rookeries joined together at the roost and occasionally they were joined by rooks who had flown south for winter. Albie knew there was a pair who had flown over a great moving water from a cold land to spend the winter at the roost. They kept to themselves, shunning the safety of the group and fending for themselves. This meant they did not have the advantage of sharing food found by one of the group but they were left alone. They could sometimes be seen a short distance away from the Stones. Albie knew why they behaved like this. Kai was pied - some of his big primary wing feathers were white. As part of a group he might have suffered at the beaks of his peers but he and his mate were happy to keep apart.

When he heard how Albie sat on the hand of a featherless one, Kai told him a story from his own land. It was a story of two ravens, larger cousins of rooks, called Hugin and Munin - Thought and Memory. They flew all over the world to bring information to a raven-god called Odin.

BELLE

Belle was the daintiest of rooks. She was very gentle and sometimes would shyly sidle up to the featherless one. She was happy to just sit there, while Albie kept flying onto the feeder's hand before then taking off to bury his cache. Sometimes she got tired of waiting for him and would fly up herself. That made Albie cross but she was his mum so he did not argue. Instead, he sat on the grass impatiently hopping from one foot to the other until she had finished. She took her time. She delicately peeled the skin from the peanuts, broke the nut into small manageable pieces before eating them. Now that it was winter she was never far from the featherless one.

It had been cold in the night and the lichens that grew on the stones and the grass blossomed white with frost. The water that pooled in crevices on the fallen stones, where the rooks usually drank, was solid ice. Once the featherless ones had broken the crust of ice in a sheep trough, Belle flew over for a drink.

Later, when the sun came out it was warm, especially sitting on top of the big stones in a sheltered spot. Belle flew up to the top of the tallest stone with her mate - it was none other than Bo. They sat there, warming their feathers in the weak sunshine.

SNOW CAWS

At the end of each day, a few minutes after sunset, the rooks answered the caw of the gathering night, joining other flocks to fly to their night roost. They flew drunkenly, until from the stones all that could be seen was a spinning, spiralling vortex of wings. They wove their way over the field, following an invisible pull, the same pull followed by their ancestors for centuries.

Albie and Mona were huddled close together on their roosting branch. The wind was chilly and air smelled of ice. A louring sky covered the crescent moon. They slept, waking to a soundless world. The sky had cleared, it was unnaturally bright for a night lit only by a thin crescent moon.

"Caw! Caw! What's happened?" Looking down, instead of grass there was a blanket of white. "What is it?" Their quiet voices woke others around them.

"It's snow!" cawed an older rook. The day was getting lighter and soon it was time for the roost to take flight for their day territories. The stones looked magical, all covered in snow. The jackdaws had already been out playing in it. Hares, too, had been jinking across the fields, leaving patterns of their paw prints. Albie flew down onto it and found it held his weight. It was very cold on his claws. He investigated it with his beak. He drew a little groove in the snow with it. It was soft and fluffy. He flapped his wings in it, as though he was having a dust bath. Showers of snow flew around him. He sank into it, flapped his wings and left a rook print.

All too soon the weak sun had melted the snow away but it had been good fun while it lasted.

ROOKERY

Hazelnut lambs' tails and willow pussy paws were blooming on the low trees beneath the rookery. Above, the rooks were building twig nurseries. Albie and Mona were very proud of the nest they had built at the top of the still leafless beech tree, close to other nests, where they themselves had been raised. Admittedly Albie had robbed other nests of building material to save himself the trouble of flying around and had occasionally been mobbed for his efforts. Unbeknown to him, his peers had returned the favour. Now Mona was happily sitting in it, looking out towards the Stones. Albie flew onto a branch above her and cawed twice.

"Kaaa! Kaaa!" Mona ignored him, too busy admiring her nest, so he hopped down so he was level with her. He bent his legs and stretched out his neck so that his beak was level with hers. He bowed and postured all to no avail.

"Kaaa. Kaaa." He fanned his tail out. Still Mona ignored him. He flew off and found her some tasty food. Bringing it back to her soon got her attention. A lot of wing beating arose in gratitude.

Once Mona had laid her eggs, she settled herself on them and Albie proudly brought her food at frequent intervals. She flew off the eggs to greet him and flapped her wings in great excitement, taking the food greedily and making a throaty "aa-aa-aa-aa-aa" noise. Sometimes she gobbled the food straight from his pouch, which stretched down from between his lower beak bones. The only other time she got off her eggs was when Albie was there to make sure nothing stole them and then only for a quick fly round to stretch her wings or to hop up and down a nearby branch. On her return, she arranged the eggs comfortably before settling down on them once more.

There had been a new crescent moon the night before the eggs hatched. Mona flew off, shrieking caws.

A-A-Albie! A-A-Albie! They've hatched!" Albie flew back to the nest with her to admire the new chicks. She sat happily crunching pieces of broken egg shell. His food deliveries doubled in frequency. Mona flew out to meet him each time he returned to the nest.

"I got the food. I decide who gets it first and you'll have to wait." Mona was not pleased. However she was hungry and when Albie finally gave her food, she flapped her wings gratefully.

"Albie, the nest needs cleaning." Albie didn't complain but cleaned up after the chicks. It was not until the moon had swelled to half its full size that Mona left the nest and its precious contents to help Albie find food for their fast growing youngsters.

SOLSTICE

It was hot. The hardest of the work of bringing up a family was over and the birds were able to enjoy the heat. It made the rooks feel soporific. Albie and Mona were sitting on the five thousand year old henge bank which circled the great stones of Stonehenge, spreading their wings to absorb the sunshine. Several other pairs were there too. They contorted themselves into strange shapes - so that the visitors were constantly asking the featherless ones if they were alright.

The Summer Solstice was fast approaching. On that one night of the year, people gathered at Stonehenge all night, as they had done since the stones had been raised. The climax was, clouds permitting, the sight of the sun rising over the Heel Stone, the stone standing apart from the other stones and which marked the alignment.

It did not inconvenience the rooks, who still returned at night to the stick nurseries they had built to raise their young. These were in the small wood on the rise between the stone monument and its visitors' centre. As it grew dark, the night was filled with strange sights, sounds and scents. The rooks watched as people migrated towards the stones, through the field, through the wood beneath them. They heard the beat of drums. They smelled a waft of the midsummer scent of elderflowers. They sensed the magic of the night. A full moon ensured it did not get dark. People came and went constantly and in the half light, they were a current of souls drifting by that could belong to any era - past, present or future.

The rooks could see from their vantage point people going right into the centre of the stones. They could feel the energy of the people merging with the power of the stones until the night pulsated with it. As the sky lightened, everyone expectantly faced the direction of the anticipated sunrise, as they had done for thousands of years. So did the rooks in their twig beds. As the first sliver of sun was about to appear, the gathering went quiet - until at the first glimpse there was a huge cheer, spreading through the watchers like a murmuration of starlings, an ancient response to the appearance of the sun.

By the time the last of the revellers were leaving, the rooks had flown back to the stones, joining the jackdaws, to see what tasty crumbs had been left. They understood the offerings to be for them as Guardians of the Stones.

By the author of

Stonedaws
- the Jackdaws of Stonehenge

Stonehenge Experience
- A Guide Through Millennia of Building Monument and Legend

and
Merlin
- the Shaman of Stonehenge

Printed in Great Britain
by Amazon

79459461R00018